A Practical Guide for Understanding

"The Fruit of the Spirit"

Introduction Booklet

by Dr. I. Franklin Perkins

dp Rochelle
PO Box 9523
Hampton, Virginia 23670
1(757) 825-0030
ItsmeDrIFP.org

© 2014 Dr. I. Franklin Perkins. All Rights Reserved

No part of this book may be reproduced, stored in a retrieval system, or transmitted by any means without the written permission of the author.

First published by dpRochelle 11/28/14

ISBN: 978-0-9862389-0-1

Printed in the United States of America
Hampton, Virginia

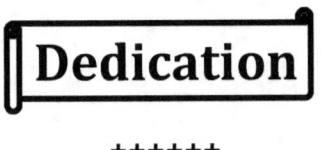

++++++

Dedicated to those who desire to redirect their energy towards their destiny.

Acknowledgments

Special thanks to my husband,
Pastor Derrick, Sr., my son Derrick, Jr.,
and my daughter Aegious,
for their offbeat inspiration.

"I love you guys the most!"

Thanks to:
Candace Shoates
Rev. Dr. Arnita Snead Brooks
Rev. Dr. Geoffrey V. Guns
Rev. Dr. William D. Tyree, III

Preface

Have you ever awaken in the morning with a notion that seemed impossible to accomplish? Perhaps you have. However, let me share with you my experience, consequently initiating the genesis of this booklet series.

During this time, I was in the middle of several projects when God dropped the idea in my thoughts to write a series on the fruit of the Spirit. Because there were already other endeavors churning, I was concerned about starting a new venture that required more of my time hence I knew this was not anything that I would have conjured on my own.

It took about two weeks to complete this work and I am spiritually better because of the intuitive illumination garnered in the process regarding the fruit of the Spirit. It is with this thought in mind that each volume will reflect this growth.

Although there are a variety of books written about characteristics and spiritual maturity, it is my aspiration to share what I call the "everyday" side of this phenomenon in layman's terms. It is a guide to judge yourself and to take an introspective glance at your spiritual walk.

It is with sincerest desire that this material may be used as a personal devotional, for study groups and book clubs, Bible study or church school sessions. A section for journaling is included so that you can jot down those insights you receive from the Holy Spirit.

It is intended to be a practical quick read in order to reach the masses on any level of comprehension. Jesus exercised practicality in His preaching and teaching and many were saved, set free, and delivered as a result. Therefore, it is my desire to do likewise.

This introduction booklet will be followed by nine subsequent booklets each expounding on the individual fruit: *Love, Joy, Peace, Patience, Kindness, Goodness, Faithfulness, Gentleness, and Self-Control.* While we are preparing the material, we ask that you would patiently abide with us as we develop these resources for your personal enrichment.

Foreword

It is a deep honor for me to have been asked to write the foreword to this powerful little booklet about the fruit of the Holy Spirit. I have had a deep interest in the spiritual life for more than thirty-five years. This book is one of the rare pieces on a vital biblical topic. Spirituality is one of the great buzzwords of the twenty-first century. Men and women of all ages, cultures, and backgrounds are craving for intimate contact and relationship with the eternal God. Each Sunday local churches are running over with people who are craving to know God and cultivate a deeper relationship with Him. The key to developing an intimate relationship with God is through our daily walk of faith and living according to His Word. Paul reminded the Corinthians that when we acknowledge Jesus Christ as Lord and confess our sins, we become new creatures in Him. The question is - what does that new man or woman look like?

Dr. I. Franklin Perkins has written a powerful pamphlet that helps believers understand and appropriate what it means to exhibit life lived under the power of the Holy Spirit. Her booklet, ***A Practical Guide for Understanding The Fruit of the Spirit:***

Introduction Booklet is a welcome addition to the body of work on the fruit of the Holy Spirit. It is not just theological and biblical exposition, moreover it is practical. This is an indication that we apply the truths that are set forth. She begins by stating that many people make the mistake of wanting to see the fruit as "fruits of the Spirit." Together all nine individual fruit form the essence of what it means to manifest the presence of the Holy Spirit in our lives. As she so ably points out all believers manifest all of the fruit in their lives. If one is going to develop the character of Christ and needs a model for growing spiritually, than here it is. She points out how the Lord will bring people into your life who are just the opposite of the character trait you are attempting to develop.

The Introduction Booklet is the first of nine future booklets, each covering one of the individual fruit. In this edition she whets our appetite for more understanding and ways that we can live out this powerful presence in our lives. Dr. Perkins skillfully defines each fruit and then prepares us for the next step in our study. The chapters are filled with biblical references and explanations that help us understand that particular fruit. Each booklet will take us deeper into the realm of the spiritual life and elevates our walk, talk, and service for Jesus Christ.

Every believer should make this series a part of their personal library and study. God has called us to a deeper life of faith and service to Him. How can we tell whether or not we are living in the power of the Holy Spirit? Jesus said that by their fruit you will know them.

Geoffrey V. Guns
Senior Pastor
Second Calvary Baptist Church
Norfolk, Virginia

Table of Contents

Introduction: The Fruit of the Spirit

Chapter 1   Introduction-Love

Chapter 2   Introduction-Joy

Chapter 3   Introduction-Peace

Chapter 4   Introduction-Patience

Chapter 5   Introduction-Kindness

Chapter 6   Introduction-Goodness

Chapter 7   Introduction-Faithfulness

Chapter 8   Introduction-Gentleness

Chapter 9   Introduction-Self-Control

Exit   Such There is No Law

References

A Practical Guide for Understanding

"The Fruit of the Spirit"

Introduction Booklet

Introduction
Galatians 5:22-23
But the fruit of the Spirit is love, joy, peace, patience, kindness, goodness, faithfulness, gentleness, self-control: against such there is no law. ESV

The fruit of the Spirit are often misrepresented as "*fruits* of the Spirit." Vines Complete Expository Dictionary uses the Greek word *karpos* which states that these united characteristics are employed by the "invisible power" which is the Holy Spirit, in the lives of those who have accepted a personal relationship with Christ. It is to this end that it is impossible to have the fruit of the Spirit or be abundantly fruitful absent the connection with Jesus as Lord and Savior.

Many times we look for various guides that will assist us with character building, spiritual formation and development training however I have not found a better genre that supersedes this list of collective personalities. Paul, the apostle, classifies these characters as "fruit" which by distinction would "make mankind fruitful" in character, and to prosper in celestial things, which is opposite with the listed "works of the flesh" that are found in Galatians 5:19-21. A tree is known by the fruit that it bears (Matthew 7:16).

Therefore, the process dictates, if you need to develop the character of love in your life, you will often entertain those who are not lovable; if you need to develop the character of joy, many that are depressed will cross your path; if you need to develop peace, those who are in torment will dominate your presence; if you need to develop patience, you will often have to wait a little longer for a few things to happen that are beyond your control; if you need to develop kindness, many rude people will don your doorstep, which will give you the opportunity to be polite; if you need to develop goodness, you will have much occasion to combat selfishness but instead accomplish nice things for others; if you need to develop faithfulness, you will come in contact with those who are not loyal or trustworthy while giving you the opportunity to demonstrate that you are trustworthy and loyal; if you need to develop gentleness, you will be faced with the irregularities of rough and harsh interactions to polish your gentleness skills; if you need to develop self-control, you will encounter situations that will demand that you can control yourself, such as with addictions and the like. Basically, you will be tested with the opposite depiction of the fruit that your life should produce.

In light of this, it is necessary to expound on the various facets of spiritual behaviors in the framework of its individual function in the group of fruit. We will address the various categories as it relates to the context of Scripture, beginning with *Love*, often underestimated yet essential to the life of the believer; *Joy*, sometimes misunderstood as happiness, yet powerful when applied appropriately; *Peace*, not frequently sought after yet often misdiagnosed as external quietness but it is rather an internal tranquility; *Patience*, not always attractive yet a quality that will prove to be an ample investment over time; *Kindness*, occasionally used discriminately yet yields a conducive atmosphere of politeness towards others; *Goodness*, not only exhibited in the actions towards others but also in the deeds accomplished for them; *Faithfulness*, trustworthiness and loyalty to promises that are made; *Gentleness*, mildness that smothers retaliation and anger; *Self-control*, temperance and strength to deny the sinful pleasures or responses previously desired. These traits do not flow from the nature of man, as does the operations gifts (motivational gifts – Romans 12:6-8), but from the nature of the Holy Spirit who produces and cultivates them in our lives.

#8

Consequently, we will review a variety of literature that will identify helpful tidbits of how "the fruit of the Spirit" is not only relevant to Christian living but also obligatory if one is to maintain a harmonious life of wholeness and satisfaction since these qualities represents the attributes of God. When we walk in the Spirit, the focus will no longer be on the desires of the flesh, it will bring enlightenment as focus is shifted from the non-essential to the necessary.

Chapter 1

INTRODUCTION - LOVE
1 John 4:7-8
"Beloved, let us love one another: for love is from God; and whoever loves has been born of God and knows God. Anyone who does not love does not know God, because God is love." ESV

Love-what a strong emotion! The Greek usage is agape – unconditional love given by God. Many times we use the word "love" as it relates to items and situations without any reservation but the use becomes rather diminished when it relates to people. We tend to throw in a happy medium such as the word "like" in order to relieve ourselves of the responsibility of loving people. It has been discovered that we can easily say we love those who love us or do things for us; however, we have disdain or in its correct form, hatred, for

#10

those who do not meet our standards only because they have wronged us in some way. Love does not mean that we must be the best of friends with everyone, it is simply an understanding that we would treat them in the way God commands us to treat others.

Unfortunately, we forgot that Jesus loved us so much that He gave His life to ensure that we would have eternal life. He did not allow the fact that we were sinners stop Him from His plan (Johns 3:16); He loved in spite of our current or even future situations.

Because of this ultimate love scenario we are given the perfect example of how to show love and when to show love to others . . . that would be, all the time.

This does not imply perfection on our part as we continue to grow daily yet we are required to love even without adequate reciprocation. We are not responsible for how others treat us but we are held accountable for how we love others. It is important to God that we learn to love both believers and unbelievers; if we do not love others, it is obvious that we do not have a relationship with Him, because God is love.

If we are to live a life of wholeness, we are commanded to love each other because love is the nature of God. It is our responsibility to show love to all people with which we come in contact whether or not they have wronged us in any way,

#12

regardless of their demographics, geographical, physical or financial status; God holds us accountable. Love is the foundation on which Christianity is built and is the glue that holds everything else together. We must never underestimate the power of love and should activate it every day. It is to this end that we will explore the four types of love.

To be continued in the booklet LOVE, Volume 1 . . .

Chapter 2

INTRODUCTION-JOY
John 15:11
"These things I have spoken to you that my joy may be in you, and that your joy may be full." ESV

Joy or delight. The Greek usage is *chara* – inner excitement that is not energized by any outside source. As a deliverance minister, many times I have the opportunity of ministering to individuals who are being oppressed and attacked by demonic forces. When someone who has symptoms of depression and suicidal thoughts asks for prayer, it usually means that joy is one of the fruit that is missing in the life of the individual. Joy offsets the onslaught of depression, sadness and sorrow.

#14

It is the devil's job to do all he can to keep us sad, powerless, unproductive and fixated on sorrow and situations of life. After all, his job description is *"to steal, and to kill, and to destroy"* but Jesus came that we would have an abundant life (John 10:10), to ensure that His joy is in us and that our joy is full because of His presence.

When the joy of the Lord is present in the life of the believer, it will be evident when they are able to rejoice in the midst of adversity that was originally arranged for their demise. Consequently, the joy that they possess is an internal joy that is locked in place to handle any type of devastation. Many at this stage fail the test because their focus is more so on things that bring a temporary form of false contentment. For when those things are gone or taken away, all of the pleasure of those things also goes away ultimately leaving the individual devoid of true joy.

Joy, when experienced brings with it an indescribable excitement that one cannot buy from anywhere in this world. The unspeakable joy that my grandmother would sing about is of the Holy Spirit. This does not imply that life will be easy or without hardships and trouble but it is how one reacts to the hardships and troubles that develops the individual into a person that is used of God and has the mind of Christ.

We cannot look to ourselves or even the things that we do to promote joy,

#16

for our works will be of the flesh absent the Savior. Paul admonished the saints at Corinth that his joy was bubbling over even though great afflictions and trials had come his way. He was not defined by the trials that persisted but developed by the trait of joy (2 Corinthians 7:4), and your hope is of the same prescription, no need to allow sorrows and burdens to rob you of your joy.

To be continued in the booklet JOY, Volume 2 . . .

Chapter 3

INTRODUCTION-PEACE
John 16:33
"I have said these things to you, that in me you may have peace. In the world you will have tribulation. But take heart; I have overcome the world." ESV

Peace is bringing together things in harmony that are divided. The Greek usage is *eirene* – an inner experience of rest. A serene disposition that is void of confusion or disturbance. Have you recently applied for a job and not sure if you would be selected? Is your body wrecked with pain or disease? Do you worry about all your bills that are due but have little money left in which to pay them? Are you up all night trying to figure out what to do about tomorrow? Are the majority of your thoughts clashing with each other in your head? If you answered yes to any of these questions, then you, my friend, are in need of peace.

Many times we are involved in events of life that do not always end as we would hope or count on things that does not come through for us but we are instructed to trust God throughout the process understanding that His peace will bring harmony in the midst of chaos. It is the peace of God that will house an overwhelming calm that will enable our spirits to be at rest when things around us are out of control.

Peace is a place of internal tranquility that implies that all is well even if outward circumstances dictate otherwise. We must allow our hearts to be reconciled with God to produce this type of fruit in our lives.

Jesus pronounced this internal peace over the woman with the issue of blood after she received healing for the disease that governed her body for twelve years. Although she experienced a rather difficult phase during her lifetime, she was able to go in peace. She could then live a life of tranquility after her issue was healed nevertheless, the peace of God surpasses all understanding (Philippians 4:7) was her calm.

In troubled times, we cannot afford to lose our minds or our ability to remember who gives us peace. It is the assignment of the devil to make us feel overwhelmed and confused but we must keep our mind focused in the peace of God which is perfect (Isaiah 26:3). We can be assured that our minds can rest independently of disturbance because we are promised that peace can be our portion (John 16:33).

To be continued in the booklet PEACE, Volume 3 . . .

Chapter 4

INTRODUCTION-PATIENCE
Colossians 3:12-13
"Put on then, as God's chosen ones, holy and beloved, compassionate hearts, kindness, humility, meekness, and patience, bearing with one another and, if one has a complaint against another, forgiving each other; as the Lord has forgiven you, so you also must forgive." ESV

Patience is another word used for longsuffering. The Greek usage is *makrothumia, makro* – long distance; *thumos* – temper, passion; to be able to hold ones temper for a long time and able to endure without retaliating. It is a matter of forbearing with persons or issues while containing your feelings in a way that you will not be offensive. Sometimes patience may suggest that one would have to learn how to deal with unprofessional or foolish behavior from others while not taking

#22

their shenanigans personally. We should remember how longsuffering God is with mankind and He does not treat us as our sins deserve but He is patient with us.

Since we live in a society that wants everything yesterday at 9:00 o'clock, more people are becoming less patient and more irritated with each other. We honk horns when someone drives too slowly, we drive with road rage for no reason, we are snappy and sarcastic with people over the phone; no one wants to wait patiently without an attitude for anything. The downside to this malady is that the lack of patience leads one to rush through necessary steps which cause a larger challenge somewhere down the line. God desires us to exercise patience with others and not to be anxious for anything that we crave (Philippians 4:6) knowing that He will bring it to us in His time.

If there is fruit development that I struggle with the most, it would be patience. Many times, I want things to move at the rate in which I can fathom the thought. Unfortunately, I grow increasingly frustrated working with others who do not process thoughts as quickly as I and sometimes get rather sarcastic when things do not happen as quickly as I desire. Too often I am faced with unwelcomed challenges that are consistently designed to develop my patience yet I am encouraged, since my patience is better today than it was last

#24

year. I am learning by each unique lesson to produce better fruit.

To be continued in the booklet PATIENCE, Volume 4 . . .

Chapter 5

INTRODUCTION-KINDNESS
Ephesians 4:32
"Be kind to one another, tenderhearted, forgiving one another, as God in Christ forgave you." ESV

When kindness is shown, all parties involved can feel the effect of this action. The Greek usage is *chrestos* - what is profitable, useful and to supply what is needed; charo – to loan, furnish or lend; a manner in which displays valuable and positive virtues towards others. It is being intentionally gracious and compassionate to those who may treat you harshly or others in general. Kindness is treating others politely when there is not any reason to do so or there is nothing that one can benefit for the politeness that is shown.

#26

In Scripture we read where Jesus showed amazing kindness to the poor, the brokenhearted, the captives, the downtrodden, the blind and bruised (Matthew 14:14) knowing that they had nothing to offer Him in return. As he displayed kindness to the multitudes, His ministry maintained a reputation of consistency. He poured out His compassion upon as many as would receive it; we are called to do likewise.

Since it does not cost a penny to be kind we should practice this spiritual art as often as the opportunity presents itself. It does not take much effort to display a heart of generosity; it is as simple as remembering the kindness of Jesus and then begin to build on His premise as the foundation. We cannot limit or reduce kindness merely as a morally good personality or a nice gesture of sorts for anyone would be able to mimic the gestures thinking that it is a formula to deceive. However, it is a virtue, a character trait that only the Holy Spirit can produce with an effective outpouring that reaches extraordinary depths.

We have little excuse not to be kind one to another (Ephesians 4:32), regardless of the circumstances; it is our purpose, it is our calling and it is our duty. Lest we miss the entire intention, we cannot believe that God's kindness will overlook our misdeeds or the adverse way in which we may treat others because He

#28

will not blink at our sin. Even in His kindness, He is just.

    To be continued in the booklet KINDNESS, Volume 5 . . .

Chapter 6

INTRODUCTION-GOODNESS
Romans 15:14
"I myself am satisfied about you, my brothers, that you yourselves are full of goodness, filled with all knowledge, and able to instruct one another." ESV

Goodness is being righteous to God and ethical in moral character to our fellowman. The Greek usage is *agathos,* a character which is good which has benefits of being actively generous in all things and profitable to others; a temperament or moral character that manifests a spirit of excellence with regard to effectively serving others by virtue of spiritual will. It is having the decency to be concerned about the welfare of others while maintaining the integrity of their interest which develops a quality that is operational.

Consequently, the misconception that being morally good is enough or equal to the spiritual fruit of goodness will not sustain in the more daunting stages of life. We know that morally good people steal ink pens and toilet paper from their jobs and play Robin Hood on the behalf of the poor, which is to take from the rich and give to the poor because the rich will not miss it since they have so much. This is the type of behavior that produces rotten fruit in an individual and will cause them to run out of spiritual gas. However, if endurance is the desire, it will require the goodness that only the Holy Spirit can produce in believers that will supersede a morally good character and harvest an effectual end result.

This explanation is indicative of Paul's message to the saints at Rome. He shares with them that he is convinced that their hearts were already pure before the Lord and that their knowledge was working in conjunction with their pure hearts. It is to this end that he reminds them to use what they have to advise those who are not living a life of wholeness of the pending danger that they would suffer as a result of not following the Gospel of Christ (Romans 15:14). It is our responsibility to pray that the Spirit would manifest goodness in our lives
 (2 Thessalonians 1:11).

To be continued in the booklet GOODNESS, Volume 6 . . .

Chapter 7

INTRODUCTION-FAITHFULNESS
Matthew 23:23
"Woe to you, scribes and Pharisees, hypocrites! For you tithe mint and dill and cumin, and have neglected the weightier matters of the law: justice and mercy and faithfulness. These you ought to have done, without neglecting the others." ESV

Faithfulness – allegiance. The Greek usage is *pistis* – which is often used of the faith that saves through grace (Ephesians 2:8) that brings about conviction of the heart based on hearing the word of faith in Christ; however, this faith applies a different meaning through the same use of the Greek word in the original language. This faith is one that is of fidelity, devotion, and loyalty. These qualities are of persons who are trustworthy and reliable in all matters. It is often that we will encounter

#34

people who intend to imitate this fruit by giving their word and making promises to all but fail to follow through, only to leave empty words that do not cover their tracks. These types of people cannot be trusted nor are they able to be counted among the dependable. In spite of unreliable people, God is always faithful to us.

In Matthew 23:23, Jesus warns the scribes and Pharisees of being more concerned with things that are of little consequence but chooses not to focus on the virtues of justice, mercy and faithfulness as if these qualities are not important; however the latter should be of more concern than the things that are valued. They did not epitomize Christian behavior, but rather hypocrisy as Jesus plainly states. We must ensure that we do not overlook the characteristics of significance in lieu of our spiritual maturity.

It pleases God when we are people of faithful quality. He wants faithfulness from us and to commit to His service for the betterment of mankind. Others should be able to count on us to be discreet with private matters and loyal to those in whom we are employed. When we keep our promises it is a witness that we are exercising the fruit of faithfulness . . . it is our duty.

To be continued in the booklet FAITHFULNESS, Volume 7 . . .

Chapter 8

INTRODUCTION-GENTLENESS
1 Corinthians 4:21
"What do you wish? Shall I come to you with a rod, or with love, in a spirit of gentleness?" ESV

The Greek usage for gentleness is *prautes or praotes* – meek or mild disposition; not overwhelmed with one's personal status or prominence. It is closely related to humility and placing the needs of others above personal needs or desires. The characteristic of this fruit allows its owner to look in the face of degrading and condescending situations and smile without feeling the need for a defense or becoming resentful or bitter. This is also seen as "power under control" even if you may be tempted by others to reveal what you have or who you are.

#38

Subsequently, Jesus was tempted on the cross by one of the criminals who hung beside Him; the thief demanded that Jesus would save him and the other thief along with Himself, since He was supposed to be God. Jesus exemplified gentleness as he never attempted to uphold His deity, however, the other thief came to Jesus' defense (Luke 23:39-43) and received salvation in the process. Many times you will not have to speak up for yourself because others will come to your rescue in challenging times.

The quality of gentleness is sometimes misconstrued as weakness. I like to call it, "quiet power," which is a secret weapon. Males who personify this character are often seen as weaklings or less than a male, but what it actually reveals is that he is more of a man when he can demonstrate restraint in various deeds towards others. An attitude of gentleness cancels the spirit of pride and exhibits acceptance of the things that God allows without complaining, disagreeing or seeking revenge on the offender. Gentleness is the key to accessing unfriendly behaviors, locked hearts and the closed minds of individuals.

To be continued in the booklet GENTLENESS, Volume 8 . . .

Chapter 9

INTRODUCTION-SELF-CONTROL
2 Peter 1:6
". . . and knowledge with self-control, and self-control with steadfastness; and steadfastness with godliness." ESV

Self-control is another word used for temperance, not simply will power but spiritual restraint. The Greek usage is *enkrateia* – the authority to rule one's self. This fruit has a wide variety of forms to which self-control can be applied. It is a submission of your will to do what is right in the midst of an otherwise stressful situation. Self-control can leave permanent stains of damage and wreck your future if it is allowed to proceed unrestrained.

It is mastering the art of keeping all of your appetites such as food, drink, drugs and sex under control. It requires one to manage their temper and various passions in moderation. Sometimes we relinquish our self-control to overeating, oversleeping and indulging in behaviors that are unseemly to those who profess Christianity; however we must submit our mind to the Word of God in order to keep our thoughts, actions and what we say in line. We are sometimes negligent in the care of what we allow to enter our spirits, perhaps through television, radio or even daily conversation. We should guard our hearts (Proverbs 4:23) and minds that we will not be overtaken by the sinful pleasures of our environment. Because too often our thoughts have a tendency to exalt itself above the knowledge of God (2 Corinthians 10:5), we are instructed to bring into captivity every one of them into obedience to Christ, since He is the only One who can do anything about them. It is then that we will be able to exhibit self-control with help from God even though we are powerless in our flesh against demonic activity.

Although the devil is often blamed for the downfalls of man, he is not responsible for the lack of man's self-control. He often suggests sensual ideas and mouthwatering opportunities to derail the individual from their purpose, which causes many to say that the temptation is too strong to avoid or even overcome. We are responsible for our own response to temptation (James 1:14) and should cease to blame others when we yield to sin. With

#44

this idea in mind, it is any wonder that there is little success with self-governance; however, what is necessary is a mind renewal in order to reduce permanent destructive behavior. No one can make us lose our temper, eat or drink too much, yield to illicit sex or compromise who we are without our permission. We surrender our control when we concede to the foolish actions of others making our fruit unproductive.

To be continued in the booklet SELF-CONTROL, Volume 9 . . .

Exit

...Such There Is No Law...
Galatians 5:23b
...against such things there is no law. ESV

There is no law divine or human that says these things are wrong. There are laws; however, that prohibits things that are illegal and flesh driven but none of the virtues can be condemned for the works of yielding fruit. Even when someone tries to imitate and develop their moral character without the Spirit, it is not any comparison to the cultivation of the believer who walks in the Spirit. Subsequently, we must note that the moral law was never intended for those who are righteous but for those who advocate lawlessness and anarchy. So, the law will judge them accordingly. Those who honor the Word of God are not under the law that governs morality but rest on a higher plane led by grace.

    Consequently, the nine fruit of the Holy Spirit work in conjunction with the believer to mold us to be the person that exemplifies Christ from the inside out. The fruit counters the works of the flesh (Galatians 5:19-21) that are in direct opposition of the Spirit and causes the fruit to activate. We cannot pick and choice which fruit we desire as they are a collection of attributes that reflects godly temperaments. To desire one and neglect the others will be an imbalance in Christian spiritual formation. We are to strive to work in concert with the Holy

Spirit in order to produce the fruit that will empower our service to others and to enhance our character as disciples of Jesus Christ.

Journaling

_____

_____

_____

_____

_____

_____

_____

_____

_____

_____

_____

_____

Journaling

_____

_____

_____

_____

_____

_____

_____

_____

_____

_____

_____

References

English Standard Version

Fruit of the Spirit,
http://www.Biblestudytools.com.
(accessed on November 4, 2014).

Fruit of the Spirit,
http://www.biblehub.com.
(accessed on November 4, 2014).

Perkins, Iris F. *Deliver Me From. . .*
Bloomington, IN: Authorhouse, 2005.

Vines, W. E., Merrill F. Unger, William White, Jr., *Vine's Complete Expository Dictionary,* Nashville, TN: Thomas Nelson Publishers, 1996.

Order Information

To contact Dr. Perkins for preaching, teaching or speaking engagements, visit the website at:

ItsmeDrIFP.org

You may also order paperback books, sow seeds and/or view itinerary at the above website.

Follow us on Twitter: ItsmeDrIFP

Mailing Address is:

Dr. I. Franklin Perkins

PO Box 9523

Hampton, VA 23670

757-825-0030

About the Author

Dr. Perkins is an ordained minister of the Gospel and effectively preaches and teaches the Word of God to the masses domestically and abroad. She serves in ministry with her husband, who is the pastor at Shalom Baptist Church, Newport News, VA. Faithful to the call, Dr. Perkins is a motivational speaker, musician, psalmist and business owner. She is also the author of *"Deliver Me From..."* and also a member on the Board of Directors at Providence Theological Seminary, Norfolk, Virginia.

She has academically prepared herself with: an ASB in Business Management, Penn Foster College, Scranton, PA; a BS in Business Administration and a MBA in Public Administration, Columbia Southern University, Orange Beach, AL; a MA in Practical Theology, Regent University, Virginia Beach, VA; a Doctorate in Ministry, United Theological Seminary, Dayton, OH; and currently working on a PhD in Management-Leadership and Organizational Change, Walden University, Minneapolis, MN. Dr. Perkins is also an instructor in the Gifts of the Holy Spirit, Christian International, Santa Rosa Beach; FL.

The author lives in Hampton, Virginia with her husband, their son and daughter.

Psalm 91:11-12

www.ingramcontent.com/pod-product-compliance
Lightning Source LLC
Chambersburg PA
CBHW050606300426
44112CB00013B/2096